# Fairy of Disenchantment

Sun Hesper Jansen

Indie Blu(e) Publishing
Havertown, Pennsylvania

## Praise for *Fairy of Disenchantment*

"Sun Hesper Jansen eloquently excavates both the mundane and the sublime. Many of the poems demand an intimate revelation through time and contemplation- seducing me to read them, again and again. Two words come to mind. Elegant and legendary. Sun Hesper Jansen's poems speak to what it means to be human. Subtle and charismatic- imbued with compassion, empathy, understanding- and the magic of one's soul."

—**Mary Rogers Glowczwskie**, *More Animal than Human* (upcoming)

"In this astonishingly honest collection, art, science, medicine and philosophy, pop culture and ancient wisdom blend from inside a machine taking pictures of a brain.

Connecting mortality to vocabulary, cold medical jargon slices through buttery poetic consciousness as Sun guides readers, with words, to the Underworld and back, from hospital to bedroom, train track to cubicle to beehive.

Coyotes and noodles and Witches and seasons and our own bones carry equal weight in this land, this book, and we readers get a sense that Sun is grounding us in every present moment of nowness. Sun has written it all down so that she, and we, don't forget: Every moment is sacred."

—**Amy Torok**, Co-author of *Missing Witches* and *New Moon Magic*

"Jansen's taut and economic poems show delicious tensions, her language scrappy yet elegant, treacherous yet gentle, wild yet erudite…

This is a masterful and sophisticated collection allowing for multiple readings and wonderful multi-leveled discoveries. *Meet me halfway*, Jansen seems to say, *we will journey together*. 'We are drifting/closer, satellites/ in shy orbit, querying./ Are you there?/ I am here.'"

—**Nancy Dunlop**, *Hospital Poems*

"The first of Jansen's accomplished artworks to appear, before any of her writing, conveys language and communication are obscured by MS's ravages, the body cut in half, nailed down, covered in barbed wire. Later in the poems, we learn the details of living with MS. Unbalanced living in only light or dark is utterly useless in this situation. And some magical truths, some pathways to cope, emerge, 'fairy tales don't lie and to name is to have power / over what has slipped away.' 'My Heart a Dancer' describes an astonishing scientific fact, "[m]edical imaging unveils / the life of the dancer's brain / at rest. And surprise: / there is no difference / between the idea of dance / and its execution.'

In the Prelude, Jansen admits, 'I don't like to look at myself straight-on, but more importantly, I don't like others to. Nothing is more restful than watching a person's gaze slide irresistibly away from my face, and get lost in their own reflection.' Reflections, whether on meaning or language, uncovered like the artist's peelings from the raven backgrounds in some of her accompanying visual art, is the book's gift to you."

—**Suzette Bishop**, *Jaguar's Book of the Dead*

"While Jansen's focus on her diagnosis of MS and how this propelled her into writing about chronic illness and lived experience grounds this collection in reality and the tangible, Jansen also immerses the speaker and reader in a metaphorical world rich with legend, mythology and stunning pastoral imagery.

The erasure pieces and artwork play a part in this immersion too, lifting the collection and Jansen's words into a realm of beautiful creation and survival; a tribute to the power of literature and art.

And so, for me, the final line of Jansen's poem 'Sign at the Entrance to the Underworld' sums up *Fairy of Disenchantment* best: 'I am home, and know my way in the dark.'"

—**Kristiana Reed**, *Flowers on the Wall*

"Sun has written words that connect me to a spiritual world I feel around me when I walk in nature or contemplate the eternal. Especially each poem in the third section titled 'Wildness'. Not pith stuff, this.

We approach the final section, after a journey that began with the process of diagnosis, then explored the poet's backstory before wending its way into that deep spiritual rapture with nature in the third.

And here… we get what might be the highlight of a standout collection: 'Before the Wild Hunt' this is not an author going quietly into the night's darkest woods, this is a human who is embracing the lifeblood she still tastes, that still courses through her veins.

Beautiful, powerful, must be read."

—**Stephen Fuller**, *Porcelain Doll Man* (upcoming)

"The poems that make up *Fairy of Disenchantment* by Sun Hesper Jansen are poetic constellations mapping her reader's way and leading them across uncertain seas to a land of better understanding of the multiple sides of someone with a disability…

In the collection's final poem, 'The Fairy Lifts Her Glass on New Year's Eve,' Jansen writes,

'In this breath—
between cycles,
my glass, your glass,
overflow

with emptiness,
bubbling questions,
art and medicine,

and somewhere, always,
kindness.'

In the end, no matter what, there are still moments in life when a toast can be raised to all that the world provides, good or bad, because the toast is still able to be made.

*Fairy of Disenchantment* is a collection of powerfully vivid, insightful, sometimes joyful, sometimes painful poems. It belongs on every bookshelf."

—**Antonio Vallone**, Publisher, MAMMOTH books, Poetry Editor, Pennsylvania English, Associate Professor of English, Penn State DuBois

"Inhabiting a rich world of symbolism tempered with dark humour -'satisfaction is ending on a minor sixth' and meditating on 'Cyclopean horrors...driving the wrong people to suicide', we are called in to walk alongside SHJ as she shows us her finest swatches and embroiders the heavens from inky black horror to shining glory.

Hope, a love of language, a recognition of humanity not being so divorced but part of the animal kingdom, and always the capacity for bravery, beauty and hope: as 'The Fairy Lifts Her Glass On New Years' Eve- 'somewhere, always, kindness'"

—**Beverley Butcher**, Author of 'Sisterhood of Broken Dolls' from the anthology *Disturbing the Body*, @boudiccapress, March 2021

"*Fairy of Disenchantment* is a poignant poetry collection that takes the reader by the hand and guides them on a journey that begins with a mirror in the therapist's office and ends with kindness. It is a soulful narrative that enchants as much as it disenchants whilst stopping to ponder the necessity of possibility and affirmation."

—**Layla Todd**, writer & poetic voice behind *Nin Chronicles*

"From the bite and the jawline, fairies, and foxes, through the tarot, and to the stars, Sun Hesper Jansen explores the underworld in this collection of poems. These poems craft a constellation, both ancient and present, illuminating and of the night. They allow the reader to trace the lines of what it means to be human, a writer, a storyteller, in relationship, a part of a family, to grapple with the body and living with MS. These poems are feral, mythic, possessed, and at the same time tender. Sun weaves in different witnessing, references, and poignant memories and creates an invitation, a portal, a way through, but no easy answers. This crossroads of making, this cleaving, is the best of poetry. With careful word choice and crafting of lines, these poems tell a story. This manuscript tells many stories."

—**Kate Belew**, Co-author of *13 Writing Spells*

Fairy of Disenchantment
Sun Hesper Jansen, 2023
All rights reserved.

Printed in the United States of America.

No part of this book may be used, stored in a system retrieval system, or transmitted, in any form or in any means by electronic, mechanical, photocopying, recording or reproduced in any manner whatsoever without written permission from the publisher, except in the case of brief quotations embodied in critical articles and reviews.

For information, address
Indie Blu(e) Publishing
indieblucollective@gmail.com

Paperback ISBN: 978-1-951724-21-4
eBook ISBN: 978-1-951724-22-1
Library of Congress Control Number: 2023940147
Indie Blu(e) Editorial Team
Candice Louisa Daquin
Victoria Manzi
Christine E. Ray
Elijah R. Carney

# Acknowledgements

To Candice Daquin, sister soul, I owe more than I could possibly say. Thank you for your unwavering belief in me, even when I insist I'm a figment of your imagination.

To Christine E. Ray, Victoria Manzi, and the badass poets, and authors of Indie Blu(e) Publishing. Thank you for amplifying the voices of the sick, the sidelined, the dismissed, and disbelieved. I'm beyond honored to be part of this work.

To D.J., again, because. Not only have you never run away from the seething abyss of my subconscious, but you show up with a deck chair and popcorn. Thank you, gentle Scabass.

To Kerfe Roig, Robert Okaji, Jennifer Patino, Conny Borgelioen, Tremaine L. Loadholt, and my WordPress community of poets, writers, and artists. Your work and encouragement are a constant source of inspiration.

To Kate Belew, Kristin Lisenby, and all the word witches out there. Many of the poems in the 'Underworlds' section, began as exercises in the first iteration of The Bardo writing workshop, and all of them have benefited from our magical literary community.

Finally, to my family and friends and everyone who's supported me on Patreon and Buy Me a Coffee, and helped me get to appointments, and howled with me at the inhumanity of the American healthcare system, and generally kept me sane and alive during one of the roughest periods of my life. I love and thank you all.

# Dedication

This is for you, D.J.

## Contents

### I. MALADY
Disenchantment: A Prelude ................................................................... 1
You Will Have an Effective Dream ........................................................ 6
Gradient Weighted Echoes .................................................................. 7
Baclofen Dreams ................................................................................ 11
Wayward Bees .................................................................................... 12
Maggie Messer ................................................................................... 14
Berenice's Hair (For D.J.) ................................................................... 17
Deep Bite ............................................................................................ 21
Considering the Void, 5am .................................................................. 22
Chicago to Lamy, One Way ................................................................ 23
Night Terror ......................................................................................... 25
Calavera .............................................................................................. 27
Five of Pentacles ................................................................................ 28
My Heart a Dancer ............................................................................. 30

### II. HISTORY
Origin Stories, 1972 / 2022 ................................................................. 37
Defiance (for Mommo) ........................................................................ 38
Spaghetti with Dad and Mr. Spock ...................................................... 42
What Remains Must Be Tended .......................................................... 44
These Here Eyes ................................................................................ 45
Conspiracy (for Kitty) .......................................................................... 47
On the Southwest Chief, Awake ......................................................... 49
The Code of Us ................................................................................... 51

Letter to John Carroll Pollak Through the Veil ...... 54

Allowed ...... 57

The New Girl, on Friday ...... 58

Sub Nivis ...... 59

Flare ...... 60

The Midnight Sun ...... 62

Sisyphe Aux Dents De Loup ...... 64

## III. WILDNESS

Four Seasons to Be Read in the Tang Lyric Style ...... 69

Fox Magic ...... 70

Ave Coyote ...... 72

The Mud of the Rio Grande Does Not Easily Release ...... 73

Above the Gorge, Listening ...... 74

Exit, Accompanied by an Ardeid ...... 75

Full Moon and Pine ...... 76

Marcescence ...... 77

Magnolia Knows ...... 78

March Song ...... 79

Petrichor ...... 80

Fall Back ...... 81

In the Woodpile ...... 82

Lullaby for a Transplanted Herb ...... 83

Cold Comfort ...... 84

Unseen Owls, New Year's Eve ...... 85

## IV. UNDERWORLDS

Sign at the Entrance to the Underworld ............................ 91
Sonata No. 6 (for Julian Scriabin) .................................... 92
Moonchild (Mise en Abîme) ........................................... 94
In the Forest ................................................................. 97
The Unseen Speaks ..................................................... 99
The Invitation (Autumn Berries) ................................... 101
Push it Open ............................................................. 102
Danse Macabre ......................................................... 104
In the Second Circle, Soaring ...................................... 106
Small Spell ................................................................ 107
The Song of the Lindens ............................................ 108
Samhain Passage ...................................................... 110
Trying to Work Magic at the Dawn Of the Cthulhucene ...... 111
Before the Wild Hunt .................................................. 112
The Chord on Which the Old Year Ends ........................ 113
The Fairy Lifts Her Glass on New Year's Eve ................. 115

# I. MALADY

THIRD DAY
upon her back.

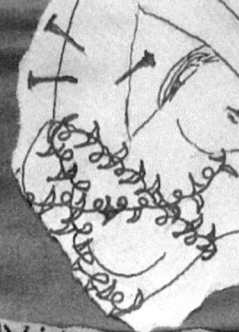

cheerfully welcomed

the devil

## Disenchantment: A Prelude

The therapist's office has a mirror. That it's behind the couch is both surprising and comforting. I don't like to look at myself straight-on, but more importantly, I don't like others to. Nothing is more restful than watching a person's gaze slide irresistibly away from my face, and get lost in their own reflection. Not that mine is an unpleasant face. It simply isn't relevant. Few people ever get past my name, if I give the one I was born with. Which suits my purpose fine. I can't believe how much of my young life was spent trying to get rid of such a powerful talisman as *Sunshine*. I might never be called upon to be anything more than a stranger's preconception.

I don't suppose, however, that I'll get away with that in this office. The situation is delicate. I want—*need*—something from this woman, and I think I know what that is. I must play along to some extent. Let her into my life, my history, as deep as is necessary. Discomfiting as her mild probing is, I answer her questions honestly, but never offer more than is asked. I'm here because my neurologist and I have determined that my depression, post-diagnosis is in need of professional attention. There is a task to complete, and I'm focused on it. I curb that side of my nature that wants to embellish. Storytelling has made trouble for me all through my life. I've avoided it for at least a decade. Until now. There's a creeping Lovecraftian novel unfolding in my brain: the unfathomable nightmare future state of Multiple Sclerosis. The therapist, if she's any good, should know that I'm playing her like I play everyone. Like I use mirrors. All my answers end with questions that shift the focus to the asker. But I'm smugly satisfied when I get her talking about her research, which happens to be on meditation.

It is 2011, years before 'mindfulness' will become so misused and mangled by dominant American culture, that I'll erase the word from my lexicon. I surprise her by knowing all the language of her specialty, although my experience of Buddhism has been a scholar's, centered on Chinese poets and philosophers. (Another story. I am not a scholar. I'm a dilettante, a rogue linguist who's been studying Chinese off and on, for close to twenty years.) But I have never practiced meditation, and we do not practice together now. She gives me homework: a CD that contains her podcast-ready contralto, guiding me through a breathing meditation, a body scan, and a *metta* meditation.

That last one, loving-kindness, I find legitimately challenging because I must offer it to myself before anyone else. I'm not allowed to skip ahead to wishing peace to my most hated nemesis. Which seems to be me. So I suspect I'll never really master that one, or the practice will just always be a bit enemy-heavy. I feel like the Buddha would approve of that.

The therapist also prescribes me something she knows I'll pursue immediately: two books. I read the first, Gil Fronsdal's *The Issue at Hand*, in one sitting. The next day, I begin the other: Pema Chödrön's *When Things Fall Apart*. The important thing about these books is not—or not only—that they have an immediately transformative effect on the apocalyptic fiction in my head. They stimulate a nerve that has been insensate for years, a muscle long atrophied. I feel like *writing*.

## Fairy of Disenchantment

I have created a blog. My first, for other people with MS. Named it *Needle Fatigue*, to alert readers from the start that this is not a place where they are required to be positive. (I am, and always will be in my heart, the Goth who in high-school French class named herself not *Soleil* but *Tristesse*.) So far on this blog, I've written a few reviews of books about MS. Some news updates related to diet and upcoming 'disease modification therapies' (a disease with no cure, can claim no 'treatments'). Today I'm attempting a bit of advice; writing a post on partially managing dizziness. My recent work with a physical therapist has given me some exercises I want to share with others. It's also summoned the indelible memory of that scene in Hitchcock's *Vertigo* in which Scotty is practicing on a stepstool in Madge's studio. (*I look up, I look down...*) I make that my feature image, and my skewed (but hopefully helpful) perspective flows from there.

*You are humorous, Jian Qing.*

My Chinese friends have called me that since the 90s, but I don't have any geographically close ones anymore. I must miss it, to call myself by that name: *Simple Clarity*. *Jian* a phonetic bridge to Jansen. The radical of my first name, *Qing*, a sun. Somehow, I respond favorably to the brightness in this language.

"Or at least *I* think I'm funny," I respond with a smirk. To myself, I think. But no. There's a surprisingly clear image floating in my mind, of a personage I've imagined often in recent days.

I took a break from my modern Buddhists to dive back into a treasured book from my budding-Chinese-linguist days, Cao Xueqin's *Hong Lou Meng*, or *The Dream of the Red Chamber*.

I've been re-reading this multi-volume Ming Dynasty epic in English (I've never been able to get far in the original) and complementing it by watching certain chapters from the Chinese TV series that was made in 1987. It's from the screen that I recognize her, the immortal known as *Jinghuan Xian*, or as David Hawkes calls her in his translation, *the Fairy Disenchantment*.

I always thought the name was perfection. I've also always been tempted to insert an 'of' before Disenchantment, because it feels like a very Goth occupation, but I know that's stretching things. The job of this fairy, or *xian*, is to awaken humans like the naive, horny young protagonist, Jia Baoyu, from a state of delusion. To dis-enchant. This is something I've been striving for. My every meditation is focused upon becoming more attuned to the here and now. Apparently, the here and now has room for celestial beings from Chinese literature.

"Hello there," I greet the fairy. "Are you here to warn me of the imminent ruin of my family? The collapse of the dynasty? To mock the folly of my passions? Or perhaps you are a muse?"

*Zuǒyòu*, the fairy says. *More or less*, in Chinese, is *left or right*.

She smiles secretively. More a feeling than a vision. Teacher and muse and alter ego, she will take many forms in the coming weeks, months, years.

She will inhabit the leaves of oolong that unfurl in hot water, and the steam rising from my cup. The ink I inject into the cartridges of my fountain pens—a symbolic reclaiming of my flesh from the syringes of Avonex. The pool of sunlight on the yoga mat where I stretch my recalcitrant muscles, so they will move another day.

She will be a ghost rooted in personal histories. A god sprung from a multitude of soils. A manifestation of a mongrel, epicurean life, nourished on myths.

She will be a raven riding a thermal up along the variegated cliffs of the high desert. A mourning dove, resting on a wire, when I return to the town full of lakes that raised me.

*Home*, as I will come to see, is wherever we happen to be.

Today, our beginning, Disenchantment has brought me a book. She waits for me to finish my blog post and puts it in my hands: *The Collected Songs of Cold Mountain*, translated by Red Pine. It feels appropriate. Han Shan was a mysterious figure, practically as mythical as the Fairy herself. It's also a book I'd completely forgotten I owned. English on one side, Chinese on the other. I will forget it again, and remember it again, as often as I forget and remember myself, and each time will feel a surge of power in the rediscovery.

Memory, as I'm already beginning to discover, is unstable, but as long as there's the potential to learn—and I *do*, something new every time I open the book—there's hope.

*Let's start here*, she says. *And see where we go.*

Sun Hesper Jansen

## You Will Have an Effective Dream

There is a poster of a white sand beach
on the wall where I watch my feet
in the mirror on the MRI machine.

It has not changed in twelve years
despite every effort to manifest
the horse that belongs there.

Dr. Haber has not said "Antwerp"
or I have lost my mind, believing
myself George Orr dreaming.

To dream effectively while awake,
you must lie so terribly still, in case
the scan is ruined by tremors.

You cannot influence the results.
You cannot conjure a horse from sand.
Yet you persist in trying.

*Fairy of Disenchantment*

## Gradient Weighted Echoes

You never forget the first time
you see the inside
of your own head.

Nor your passion for the first
radiologist who paints you
beautifully
in the language of science.

*The ventricular system and cortical sulci*

*are within normal limits.*
*There is no significant atrophy*

*or hydrocephalus.*


'Normal' and 'no' —
Your eye devours these words
with perverse zeal, considering
how fiercely you've fought them
all your life.

*Mild scattered foci*

*of increased FLAIR signal*

*are again noted*

*involving the paratracheal,*

*deep,     and     subcortical     white     matter.*

Fluid Attenuated Inversion Recovery.
You look it up, and are disappointed.

*In addition, a small focus of*

*increased FLAIR signal is noted*

*along the right aspect of the genu*

*of the corpus callosum.*

Here
is where your gaze narrows.

You stare into the shining heart
of your oldest, largest lesion.

You know it like your friends
know their ruling planets
and indeed, Mercury is all over
your chart, but not here,
in your brain, anymore.

This thing is *eating*
every one of his gifts.

## Fairy of Disenchantment

You are staring at the reason
you can't communicate,
the short-circuits that tip
the balance from brain fog
to permanent liability.

There are seven lesions, total,
wreaking a havoc too poorly
understood, to predict.

Ignorance is enough.
You caress the status quo.

*This white matter disease*
*is stable*

*when compared to the previous study.*

*No new white matter lesions*
*are identified.*


Blessed be the absent
intra-axial mass.

The inconsequential
axial fluid collection.

Your eyes blur in the rapture
of the unremarkable.

Sun Hesper Jansen

*Normal flow voids*
*are noted*

*in the internal carotid*
*and basilar arteries.*

All that you need
is in this absence.

## Baclofen Dreams

Baclofen dreams have no narrative.

I wake to the ceiling fan crashing
to the floor and sit in shock with
curses and a fantasy of plaster
in my mouth; I've traded oneiric
epics for works of flash fiction
that make me dread falling sleep.

One more price to be weighed:
to walk without pain, or rest
with more languid nightmares.

Sun Hesper Jansen

## Wayward Bees

Reaching for *that word*
through a din of synonyms,
I suddenly think of bees
in collapse, flying blind,
their minds addled in
chemical cacophony.

At what point do bees
say 'aberrant?' When
do they realize the loss
of context and direction

and what does the hive
have to say about it?

At what juncture do I
decide I'm too sick
to be of use? Fly into
my demyelination,
pollen heavy as gold
on my pointless limbs?

And in what world
could I just start building,

*Fairy of Disenchantment*

not a house of wax to
wall me up but a place
of honeyed welcome
for the wayward?

"Wayward Bees" was previously published in *But You Don't Look Sick: The Real Life Adventures of Fibro Bitches, Lupus Warriors, and Other Superheroes Battling Invisible Illness*, 2021.

## Maggie Messer

I will make excuses for them.
A walking stick is not a cane.
It resembles an affectation
particularly with a pace too fast
to explain the reality:

that I must race to keep moving,
to keep my legs from becoming
sculpture, to compensate for
the tilt and spin of my own world
and *gods* I hate a crosswalk.

I'll make excuses, but not now.
Now, I want magic: the chance
to be a superhero of the darkest kind,
Maggie Messer with a message
of educational vengeance.

I couldn't tell you the color or
make of the car, and the features
of the driver and his girlfriends
are a blur of blondness, but this
is enough for my purposes.

Next time, in an alternate world,
when I lock eyes with the driver

and point at the crosswalk, he will
stop out of shock, the screech of tires
as loud as the blood in my ears.

## Fairy of Disenchantment

The knob of my stick is solid, heavy,
and when it meets the car's windshield,
glass will spider under the glorious smash.
Mild-mannered MS-er become Messer,
a knife to your able-bodied heart.

He will get out of the car with a *What the
fuck* but this, I'm afraid, is not a dialogue.
*Do you want to know what it's like*, I'll ask,
magnificently unhinged; *to be disabled?
Would you like to know right now?*

Before he can speak, the side of his head
will meet my stick with a sickening thud.
As he crumples to the tarmac, I'll tell him
how the first time I fell in the middle of
the street, *people walked over me*.

*The stick reduced the falls, but it hasn't
reduced the assholes*, I will inform him
as he tries to rise and can't. I've made a
mess of his inner ear. *Feel dizzy?* I'll ask.
*Buck up, honey; you'll get used to it.*

*You'll mark the days that you're not dizzy,*
I'll say as the bleeding fool gets to one knee.
When I whack his leg out from under him,
I suppose his girlfriends will be shrieking,
mosquitos of conscience in my ear.

*Oh sorry, is it hard to move those legs?*
I'll ask when he tries to stand up again.

Sun Hesper Jansen

*There now, that's one more thing we have
in common, especially in the summer heat.
That's all, kids; I'm late for work.*

It is, of course, an absolutely wrong use
of superpowers and regained time. I stare
at the place my stick would be bloodied
and wonder where my real magic went,
the strength of my own steady breath.

Maggie sneers at our options: Then what?
Call the non-emergency police number,
wade through the automated menu and the
chain of people who will fail to understand
exactly what crime just occurred?

A new timeline, at the crosswalk's edge.
I watch the traffic for as long as it takes
for the sun to lay its hands on my shoulders,
for the long lack of rest and peace to sink in.
I turn my back, and call in sick.

---

"Maggie Messer" was previously published in *But You Don't Look Sick: The Real Life Adventures of Fibro Bitches, Lupus Warriors, and Other Superheroes Battling Invisible Illness*, Indie Blu(e) Publishing, 2021.

## Berenice's Hair (For D.J.)

For a night or two, in my ninth summer
I knew the names of ten star patterns,
constellations traced by my Cool Cousin,
animated in my memory like a
Terry Gilliam film.

Now, like celluloid perversely charred,
my mind sees only familiar shapes,
with burnt-out holes where names once were,
necessitating tricks of verse
to fix them into place.

Begin with the Big Dipper, which is
just the arse-end of Ursa Major;
the bear's long tail tells a story
in at least three Greek myths,
all of them cruel.

None explain why the bear is wearing
a girdle, but it's marked by Dubhe on
top of the Dipper's bowl,
and below, Merak is the mark
that points to Polaris.

Behind and below the bear, is Coma Berenices,
an asterism subtle, yet worth remembering,
a shimmering triangle representing the hair
that Ptolemy the Third's queen
sacrificed to Aphrodite.

Sun Hesper Jansen

In more ancient times it was the puffy tail
of Leo, then a lion of Bert Lahr proportions,
now just a kingly cat, the stars of its mane
forming a backwards question mark,
with Regulus at its point.

Virgo could pull Leo's tail if she wasn't so busy
representing goddesses from Athena to Demeter,
most fitting the latter, since in one hand she holds
the "Ear of Wheat," brilliant Spica—in truth
a binary star.

Curving upward from Spica, you will soon find Arcturus
and the ghost of Jack Horkheimer says I'm doing this wrong.
You start at the top, at the Big Dipper's handle,
"Follow the Arc to Arcturus, then Straight on to Spica;"
I say: whatever works.

No matter your route, you are now in Boötes,
the broad-chested herdsman who ropes seven oxen,
the stars of The Plough (yet again, the Big Dipper);
in Latin they're the Septentriones, but myself I prefer
the "Dipper Dogies."

Do not confuse the Herdsman with Hercules,
whose famous heroic torso is known as the Keystone,
formed by four stars that aren't nearly as interesting
as cluster M13, under his left armpit, holding
300,000 stars.

*Fairy of Disenchantment*

Below the Hero is fat Ophiucus, the Serpent Bearer,
or Asclepius, god of medicine, wielding a snake,
so long it makes up two constellations, Serpens Caput,
the head, in his left hand, and the tail in his right,
Serpens Cauda.

Close enough for the snake to snatch in its mouth
is Corona Borealis, the Northern Crown, whose star
Alphecca means "brightest of the broken," a phrase
sadly apt for this tawdry gift to Ariadne,
who trusted too much.

Back to Hercules, at least let me recall his neighbors;
the Summer Triangle of Cygnus, Lyra, and Aquila.
Cygnus the swan, with Deneb the star in its tail;
Albireo the "beak star" is again two stars,
one amber, one blue.

Descending from Cygnus is the tiny harp, Lyra,
whose handle star, Vega, has the meaning of "falling."
For the Chinese, Vega is Zhi Nü, the Weaving Maid,
who falls for Niu Lang, the irresistible Cowherd,
every summer anew.

At last is Aquila, forever riding celestial thermals,
its tail star Altair, linking Deneb to Vega, gives flight
to the eagle in Arabic, connotes the Cowherd in Chinese,
but to me, mainly evokes monsters, Anne Francis,
and the feckless Krell.

Sun Hesper Jansen

With luck, at least some of these mnemonics will stick
in the event some young cousin needs me to teach them.
Just for my own arcane purposes, on the off chance
fairy tales don't lie and to name is to have power
over what has slipped away.

If not, I'll invent an appealing legend to explain my loss:
that some god hurled my memory into the heavens,
where it's lodged somewhere mysterious,
deliberately unfindable, maybe tangled forever
in Berenice's Hair.

## Deep Bite

You'd be a great candidate for Invisalign®,
the dentist says, educating me as to
the depth of my bite, lamenting the
wear of anxiety on my molars, the stress
on the joints of my perma-clenched jaws.
The receptionist presents an estimate
of the anticipated out-of-pocket cost:
over five thousand dollars with my
useless, toothless insurance policy,
and I sign the form that acknowledges
my understanding of the unattainable,
that I am condemned to the dentition
of my grandmothers, and I exit with a
smile that wants nothing so much as a
neck in which to prove just how deep
a bite I have.

Sun Hesper Jansen

## Considering the Void, 5am

Reading about geology and deep time
and Norse mythology before bed
apparently means that I wake up
with a line like this in mind:

*There were tardigrades*
*in the Ginnungagap.*

I blink into the before-alarm dawn,
pondering insanity, and the vision
of the great Primeval Cow licking
a little water bear into being.

## Chicago to Lamy, One Way

tracknumber19tracknumbertrack
20tracknumber20numbertrack
number18tracknumbertrack

Don't let me miss this train again,
swimming through brain fog and the
quantum come-hither of tracknumber9

tracknumber8track—*there* is Track 8
and I break into a three-legged lope
as the red cap flies past, bearing all
those passengers unafraid to ask,
to admit they can use help.

No matter, I've won the dare again
and the first jolt of movement is
like the touch of a god, thrusting
me into another body, as graceful
as anyone here—no, I am *more*,
a sailor at home on the Railsea,
striding car to car with no cane,
while the able-bodied pitch around.

I will regret lying to the solicitous
attendant about my stick, as soon
as we reach Lamy and my limbs
question my every command,
and so, this time, I tell the truth:
I am fine, but I might not be
tomorrow, and have you heard
of a little thing called MS?

Sun Hesper Jansen

But it never takes long, a day,
to heal from it all, for everything
to reset in the red rock and the
dry heat until the stick feels almost
unnecessary, its only purpose
the same as everyone else's,
to navigate inclines and resist
the fatal pull of canyons.

Returning, there's a single track.
No confusion, no noise, just wind.
Wind and the hum of regret.

What mistake am I making, again,
going back the other way when
home is wherever I'm healthy?

A coyote trots along the rails.
Pauses in the shade, facing me.
As if watching what I will do.

"Chicago to Lamy, One Way" was previously published in *But You Don't Look Sick: The Real Life Adventures of Fibro Bitches, Lupus Warriors, and Other Superheroes Battling Invisible Illness*, Indie Blu(e) Publishing, 2021.

## Night Terror

The light of your nightmares
is a recognizable shift from
red to blue, stark and stuttering,
the faulty fluorescence of an
apocalyptic ER, a half-looted store
whose name is a banal construct,
void of personality, or hope.

The animals you dream are
wild, exquisite, and tortured;
last night you identified them as
the daemons of your human cast,
of most loved, most dreaded.
He was the arctic fox, bloodied
from one trap after another.

In the middle of the aisle where
fresh unimaginable cruelty would
make you scream yourself awake,
you watched him *leap up*, released,
and with cinematic grandeur
blow out, shatter, and evanesce
into the inhuman light.

Rabbit-hearted in the dark,
a talisman of sulphur quartz
cool in your sweating palm,
you absorbed the inevitable.

Sun Hesper Jansen

Willed yourself a respite from
random horror, and rolled over,
to rest and fight again.

## Calavera

How often do you sit

companionably
with your own skull

cradling that jaw
tenderly

feeling the indentations
of each molar

gradually sensitive
to the fragility

under your fingers,
then suddenly

sickeningly aware

that you could bust
it all apart
with just one
ferocious grab

in an ecstasy
of displacement?

## Five of Pentacles

The question of refuge
is one we fear to ask,
raised to shoulder,
to carry, to care for
anyone but ourselves.

One day
the Hanged Man
will be cut down
by the Moon.

You'll go mad enough
to see the path, dimly.
There is a steep drop
with no bottom to be seen
beneath the mists.

Listen to me.
Know there is a net
down there, beyond sight,
under swaying bridge.

When you reach
the sun-drenched ruins
on the hill, remember
you didn't come here
to be cured.

*Fairy of Disenchantment*

The solace
of this place
is simply knowing
you can stay.

## My Heart a Dancer

Evelyn Glennie
taught me to listen,
with the body, not the ears.

Connee Boswell
taught me to swing,
with the soul, not the body.

*I listen to myself,
and all I've learned:
This is not exile.
This is not torture,
watching you spin.
I move with you.*

Sing, Science,
of the persistence
of muscle memory:

Medical imaging unveils
the life of the dancer's brain
at rest. And surprise:
there is no difference
between the idea of dance
and its execution.

*My fingers follow yours,
in silent percussion.
Invisibly my floreos
stir the air.*

*Fairy of Disenchantment*

*I whirl in the tempest
of your flying skirts.*

Long ago our mothers
grounded our hearts to the dirt
our soles kicking sand
like offerings into fire.

We move with them.

*When the universe implodes,
your joy, your power will remain,
curled in your parietal lobe.*

# II. HISTORY

## Origin Stories, 1972 / 2022

She was running from the Cavalry
in that dream, me, a baby on her back
(*Little Big Man* on the screen of her mind).
I was named from a nightmare
of being hunted, yet what she recalls
most of all, was that I was speaking to her.

Whatever we say in the womb, we forget.
I'm not sure we've ever stopped running.

Fifty years later, I dream of us in a caged city
made up of women and wild creatures.
Neither and both, I flee the siege, slipping
down like a ghost through the bars, running
but not escaping, making a reconnaissance
of yet another invisible enemy.

A mountain lion lifts me up by the claws
into the last night of our captivity.

Sun Hesper Jansen

## Defiance (for Mommo)

The mirror that is seen, is almost useless,
but I know the resemblances by heart, especially
that querulous contortion of my eyes, misread
so often as anger, that answers a question or
a statement half-heard or unexpected. People;
it's nothing more than concern or curiosity, or a
challenging of unclear language; a need to fix
an unsatisfactory state of knowledge.

How many hours we clocked at the library,
working on that never-ending quest together,
I'll not know, but I can't help noticing my crib
is still lined with books, mostly science fiction,
science fact, and fantasy, novels whose caliber
would meet even your exacting tastes; everyone
knows you could teach college lit if not for
a few pesky pieces of stiff paper.

But I'm guessing you'd hate that: your words
on other people's terms, at other people's pace.
"She keeps to herself," they may say about you,
but I know this is half a lie; after the parties,
explosions of notions are the introvert's gift.
I miss the midnight dissections of Dickens,
the quantum mechanical travels, but luckily
I have your brain on speed-dial.

*Fairy of Disenchantment*

Where would half my worlds be without
your verification that they've yet to be written?
Or my ego without your anticipation of sequels
and movie rights; I'm glad you're patient about that
because my stories grow at the rate of gardens,
which you've apparently added to your long list
of artforms, after pastels, drawings, wire figures,
and Surrealist pipe-cleaner cat toys.

You're restless and bored and I dig that;
What other girl in the 70s had all her costumes sewn
from inspirations from the Encyclopedia Britannica?
What happened in the 80s, I don't want to talk about;
what decade of teenage angst doesn't strangle
the tightest mother-daughter bond? Regardless,
I blame Reagan. We've never ceased struggling,
but at least we're on the same side now.

Walking downtown I see ghostly overlays
of past-on-present. Behind the shiny windows
of apartments and offices, you and I eat burgers
at the Woolworth's lunch counter, see a movie
at the Strand; it all went away before our eyes.
I get worked up about who can afford to live there
now (Reagan again), but at least when they built
the new library, they were thinking of us.

If only our healthcare system were redesigned
with such intelligence; every day you go to work,
you navigate the rubble of a profession deformed
by greed. "Why," even I used to ask, "doesn't she
look for another job? Anywhere would be better

*Fairy of Disenchantment*

than that place." But the residents know and
so do I, your subversive compassion; if not for
your defiance, who would even care?

Going back to both mirrors, I will confess to envying
everything, really. My commitment to keeping it all
together, being responsible, and not just running off
to join the circus, has always needed improvement.
And like everyone, I've wanted that long curly red hair,
but at least after all this time, I've learned to be happy
making silk flowers for your braids, while my own
sharp blondness, bleaches in the sun.

But sooner or later you'll say, "You know, kiddo,
I've got enough flowers," so I've crimped together,
Instead, this ode to all the scrappy habits I've learned
from you, and to the fact that no one ever really knows
what's going on inside our scrunched-up foreheads.
Like I said, it's probably just that work-in-progress,
some tasty new problem. Or we could really be angry,
but man, that's a whole other poem.

Sun Hesper Jansen

## Spaghetti with Dad and Mr. Spock

Home from school again today,
"Feeling sick?" says my Dad.
I sniffle, a juvenile thespian with
maybe some kind of cold coming on,
and a nod is all I need; Dad says:
"You should probably stay home."

Curled up with my books, I drowse
until the telltale pasta pot
taps the stove; Dad wonders
if I'd like macaroni and tomato juice
or maybe some spaghetti with the
diminutive meatballs only he makes.

Dad's day-off ritual culminates
in whatever Star Trek we taped
the previous night, and well before
the histrionic singer hits that note,
I'm a caterpillar on the couch,
hot bowl of noodles in my hands.

What'll we see today, Dad? Apollo?
or the Tribbles, or Trelane?
or Jack the Ripper or Harcourt
Fenton Mudd, or the Horta, or
pregnant Julie Newmar, or maybe
The Gunfight at the OK Corral?

*Fairy of Disenchantment*

What happens to Kirk? Who cares
as long as Mr. Spock is there
to reason, doubt, and analyze,
unafraid of the bitter choices,
and absurd costume changes,
required to see the mission through?

Or will it be that sad episode
where he must break the heart of that
smart Romulan lady captain,
or leave Jill Ireland in paradise,
after hanging like a fool from a tree;
it seems logic always has its price.

But no, it's my favorite: "Mirror, Mirror"
and I get to see Uhura with a dagger,
a louche scarred Sulu, and best of all
bearded Spock, still the wise one,
his Luciferian logic intriguing
his clean-shaven counterpart.

Thanks, Dad, I might just nap here,
full of spaghetti and meatballs and
questions about alternate universes
and moralities; perhaps in the Mirror
Universe every kid stays at home
to get a quality education.

Sun Hesper Jansen

## What Remains Must Be Tended

It was a hallucination, he thought, the bodies floating
like sky divers caught on some eerie thermal, outside
the window of his hospital room, where part of him
remained. Is it because I belonged to these spaces
so young, that I could see what no one else believed:

that you never fully emerge from this crossing,
or you can, but you must work at it, with a will.

He survived, he thinks, and so did you, but this is no
trick of the light, this washing out, this layer of ash;
I snap my fingers to spark the dullness of your eyes
into flame: *Stay with me*. I don't care what disdain
it kindles, or amusement, or worry for my sanity

if I can see you draw away from what I see, beyond
the glass, the reflection returned to you, burning.

*Fairy of Disenchantment*

## These Here Eyes

They sent you to live with a strange family for half a year,
rich enough to care for a cross-eyed girl, but not as fun

as your real parents or the brother you loved and terrorized;
the story is cinematic, but the part I can never quite shake
is

the horror of knowing
that you were wide awake
during the four-hour procedure
that I can't even mention,

that gave you double-vision for a year and never liberated
you from a lifetime of cats-eyes and Coke-bottles; I cringe

at your inner canthus stretched by an epoch of spectacles,
even as the mischief that glints through the glass makes me

remember when we read
Colette and Maupassant,
and drew up ambitious blueprints
for houses beyond our means.

Those eyes recognize me sometimes, but I confess
I prefer the times when I'm a total stranger, and worthy

of your unconditional smile, the one that seems to say:
"Get me outta here, kid, and we'll go find some trouble!"

Sun Hesper Jansen

I can't help but suspect
this was the very same look
you gave that boy from the wire mill,
that lasted seventy-five years.

I think of the forty-two addresses, across eight states,
you've occupied; your visions of buildings rising and falling

must put mine to shame. I wonder if you've finally settled
into the one you loved best, or if it's one that we designed.

I'm never there to see it
but I know you take them off,
and smile like I do, solaced
by the blur of the world.

## Conspiracy (for Kitty)

This morning I froze
at a whistle: death,
a parallel train creeping
over my shoulder;
I refused to turn,
thinking of Orpheus;
stiff-spined, I let it pass;
counting empty boxcars,
and feeling a thrill,
as you might have done.
As if this passage
could be cheated.

Yesterday on the fourteen
acres I call utopia
we walked, serenaded
by the first spring frogs,
haunted by the one
solitary bat that flapped
staggering in sunlight,
grasping at gnats —
a sign at first,
then just a symbol
of another disease
willfully uncured.

Now, what I carry is
a perverse peace,
of fellowship,
of the final gift from one

Sun Hesper Jansen

who knew friendship,
who gathered
about her, a host of
splintered families,
and bound us in one
final conspiracy:
breath, and a pulse
in the jugular.

*Fairy of Disenchantment*

## On the Southwest Chief, Awake

Everyone knows the call of the train
from a distance, the lonesome howl
that pulls the heart
and sometimes
lures the body somewhere,
anywhere, away.
Those who live near the tracks
almost never hear romance
in the freighter's jarring blare,
but when the passenger trains
rattle past and whistle,
mothers and children still wave.

To those who ride, there is something
maternal, rocking, in the sideways
sliding rhythm, but only to a point.
To sleep in the belly of a
hurtling train is to borrow
its restless nature, buffeted by
lullabies of wrenching metal,
lurching speed, and memories.

Trains wail, yes,
and they wail all night,
soothing, yes, sometimes,
but more often not.
Trains rage, bellowing
like iron dinosaurs,
tearing blindly through copses
of river-fed trees.

Sun Hesper Jansen

In the desert, trains whimper
as if remembering pain,
and the rail gibbers
with the voices of dead men,
most speaking Cantonese.

In the night, trains mutter and cry out
like dreamers wanting someone
to wake them from their nightmares.
Trains are troubled sirens,
keening inconsolably,
sharing their madness,
whispering, rasping, shouting,
exhausted, rusting, wanting to sleep
and to run forever,
fast as the scrubland horses
they scatter with their shriek.

Lying awake, insomniacs listen
and imagine all kinds of things
in the murmurs, sobs, and whines,
but mostly their own desires,
the relentless impulse to movement,
somewhere, anywhere, away,
at inevitable, unknowable cost,
somehow always worth it.

## The Code of Us

If we wrote what we said,
one might think it a code

and so, we seem already
to outsiders, speaking in
anacoluthons, clear enough
to each other, mostly—

this page, torn from an
obscure imprint, is what
I saved from that voyage
of lost images, and I am
overcome

by being there again, a ghost
in Taos, looking up
that ladder that led to nowhere,

and into the blood-weeping
eyes of Nuestra Señora
de la Soledad, listening to
Blue Spruce Standing Deer
speak of his grandfather,

gathering us
into so many worlds
all at once.

Sun Hesper Jansen

This page from Gertrude Stein's
*Portrait of Mabel.*

There were more, but I kept
only this one—why?

And why these lines to spark
just one poem of us,
that code, to speak our language
which is also bent

and alone
and abandonment
and not vanishing,

letters cut

from some synchronicity,
from one of our alternate eras.

I still want them
to find one day, a trove of clues
to our escape, that last great
joke on civilization,

that masterful plan we hatched
in Glenwood Springs,

*Fairy of Disenchantment*

that would, with your luck
and my art

leave them

wondering.

Sun Hesper Jansen

# Letter to John Carroll Pollak Through the Veil

You kissed me,
then you kissed him,
to his wonderment,
lips to fingers to cheek
in a benediction both
suave and frivolous,
and that was our last
embrace in this world.

It rained that day.
Your sacrificed umbrella
lies in our foyer,
apart from the others,
so that we might trip on it
*in perpetuum.*

Because of you, no Latin
or Greek passes without you
declaiming etymologies
in my head as we weave
from the Inn of the Loretto
to our first meeting place.

All roads lead to Del Charro.

We miss you, John.
So much that you adorn
the altar of our departed,

*Fairy of Disenchantment*

handsome and casual
in Krakow.

I taste you in my
Marlborough wine,
take your bitters
with my soda water,
let your fried potatoes
sit in the skillet
because they really are,
even better cold.

Your letters are here,
your hand immortal,
your stories indelible.
I have lost the *Trilogy* but here…

Here are *Sgt. Kozak's Book* and
*The Last Thing He Wantonly Shot.*

I would release all your words
into the world, if you were only
to speak to me now, quickly,
while the veil is thin.

Or I could steal them,
just as I've purloined
your penmanship.

Your voice, though,
I could never claim.

Sun Hesper Jansen

I confine myself
to mastering the magic
of your lowercase *d*.

## Allowed

News: there is no law
against second chances.

So much is allowed.

The equinox came and
went, and September
dug its claws deep
in summer's flank.

And there, somehow,
under an improbable arbor
of grapes ready to press,

you and I went back
seven years and kissed
the world right again.

Sun Hesper Jansen

## The New Girl, on Friday

Here
is an opportunity
to reinvent oneself

with strangers

with superiors

She
must be muzzled
before she betrays

our pleasures

our poisons.

They ask
about my plans
for the weekend.

Low key.

Nothing much.

We give them
just enough
to damn themselves.

*Fairy of Disenchantment*

## Sub Nivis

Sprung from cubicle hell,
a blinking office mole,
I gasp at the suddenness
of a sky made of snow.

Entering the atmosphere,
feels briefly like drowning,

my nose and mouth fill
with feathers of ice.

Each flake is immense;
one hundred-spiked specimen
sticks to my coat like a burr.

At the bus stop, not one soul
swats the magic away.

I watch three separate girls
snap pictures with their phones.

In this shared, silent moment
of slowed molecular momentum,
we are still as snow monkeys,
lynxes, mountains, stones.

Sun Hesper Jansen

## Flare

We connect
like mediums
across a dark,
liminal space.
*Are you there?*
*I am here.*

I am afraid
of my eagerness.
We have only
been ghosts
communicating
over the wire.

But over barbs,
briars, fire,
I would jump
to reach you
if you sent up
a single flare.

In that painting
you raised a lantern.
Miranda, I thought,
on an 'isle full of
noises,' your voice
shining clear.

*Fairy of Disenchantment*

It took so long
to grasp that
our lives had been
struggling sideways,
like Orphée in pursuit,
together, apart.

Your text arrives,
subverts time,
erases miles
between us.
I shine back
the tender beam.

How is it that we
illuminate so much
while devouring
our own light?
Yet it's happening
even now.

We are drifting
closer, satellites
in shy orbit,
querying.
*Are you there?*
*I am here.*

Sun Hesper Jansen

# The Midnight Sun

I have painted, since I can remember, this melting sun,
and in every ray of bleeding oil is a face no one recalls
but me. You're making this worse, you say; you wish
I would stop, paint something/anything new, to paint
you, as if love will keep the earth from incineration.

The power you give me, when I only paint what we
have made, and I'm sorry the burning cities on my
canvases give no relief—and in the shadows, blood pools
and glaciers melt and myriad species add their bones to
the fossil record—but I can do anything now but stop.

Because nothing has felt real for so long, you believe
we inhabit The Twilight Zone. That all I need to do to
cool the world, and your frantic heart under my cheek,
is to paint a waterfall. Fall asleep and dream, this a fever,
with cool peace and reason waiting on the other side.

In November, you say, we'll wake up to a different
world. But I know my Rod Serling, and in that world
the sun's been left behind, and cool, silencing snow
falls soft as complicity, freezing blood, growing glaciers
over the fossil record, as we race into endless night.

*Fairy of Disenchantment*

I can do anything now but stop.

And you can do anything but sleep.

So wake with me, and work.

"The Midnight Sun" was previously published in *As the World Burns: Writers and Artists Reflect on a World Gone Mad*, Indie Blu(e) Publishing, 2020.

Sun Hesper Jansen

## Sisyphe Aux Dents De Loup*

*Il faut imaginer Sisyphe heureux,* **
said the Bodhisattva of the Absurd,
my protector in this ceaseless labor.

There is no end to this but the end,
and no reward. I am godless and free,
a body through which all light passes.

I could let this go, fill my pockets with
enough rubble from the ruined city,
walk into the arms of the waiting lake.

You could never withstand it, this life
you have never lived. And this alone
is enough to strengthen my back.

I grit my teeth again, in a lupine smile,
like all wild things once thought beaten,
returning time and again, to diminish you.


\* Sisyphus with Wolf Teeth
\*\* 'One must imagine Sisyphus happy', Albert Camus, *Le Mythe de Sisyphe*

# III.
# WILDNESS

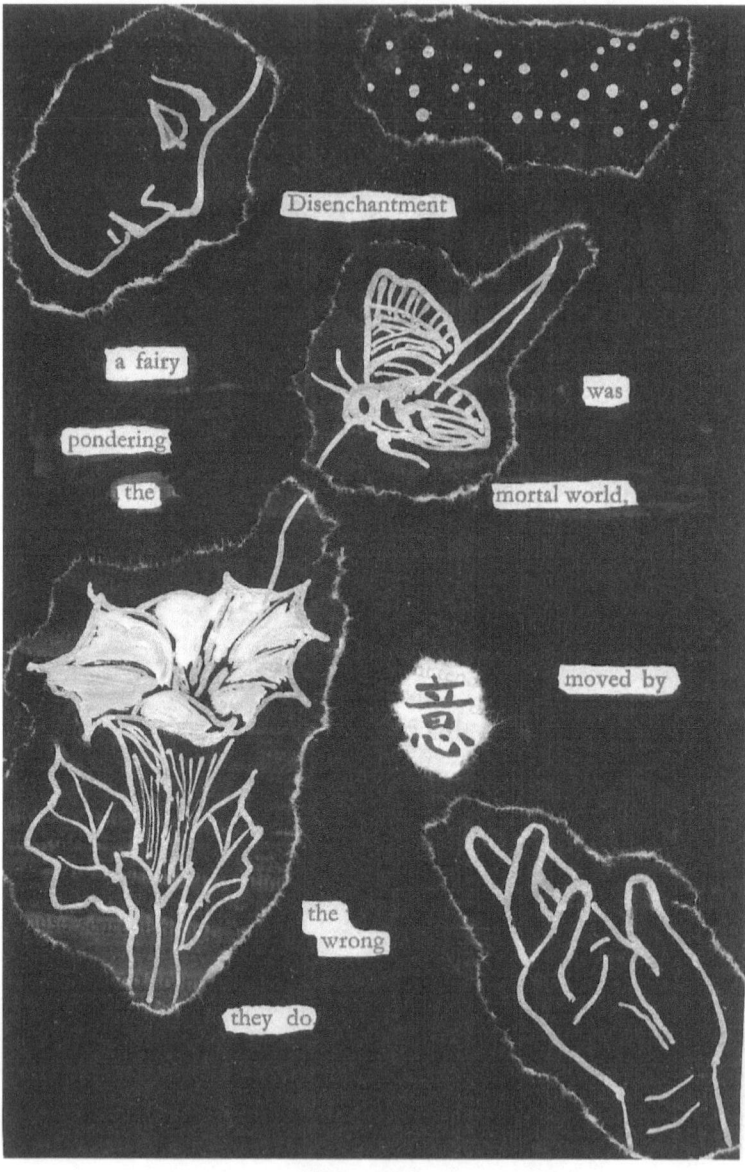

Disenchantment a fairy was pondering the mortal world, moved by the wrong they do

## Four Seasons to Be Read in the Tang Lyric Style

I.

March is cruel with dreams.
Snow-melt floods my soul,
no sun what it seems,
ice-blood cracks and steams.

II.

Long, slow hours in June,
my heart hums with bees.
Each thought falls in tune,
Each word sings of swoon.

III.

Years haunt this front lawn.
You and she, like kids,
play in leaves piled on.
That tree too, long gone.

IV.

Soft, still, no shrill cry:
snow hides one lone hawk
White plumes trick my eye.
Rapt, I watch her fly.

## Fox Magic

Foxes, legends tell us,
reveal themselves to
the foolish and fey,
malicious tricksters,

bent on magical hijinks,
cruel seducers,

cunning incarnate.

If a fox could speak,
it would laugh and ask:
What beats man for
blithe malice and cruelty?

What worse deceit
than weaving myths
to demonize wildness?

Punishment for a fool
is to see in the suburbs
this flash of russet fur,
these eyes of amber,

*Fairy of Disenchantment*

and not feel
more than magic
a mending.


Wildness
recovered.

Sun Hesper Jansen

## Ave Coyote

Up with the ravens,
one thousand feet
above the meander
of the mother river,
surefooted on slickrock
unhindered by rainfall,
we strain at the edge,
ears funneled, peering
into the lapis mist
as it trails, a veil
sedately sweeping
across miles and epochs,
condensing, careless
of our joy, into a
soft, yipping chorus
of bright canid cries.

*Fairy of Disenchantment*

## The Mud of the Rio Grande Does Not Easily Release

The mud of the Rio Grande does not easily release;
it anchors the ankles cold as the current rushes, directs
every liquid molecule to the source, even as the horizon
bruises beneath a veil of rain, spurring the heart to flight.

The kick of wind does not ruffle the birds; unhurried
they call from the basalt cliffs, careless of the spidery bolt
that severs and sutures heaven and earth. Untethered
in time, dry-feathered, they dive and catch while they can.

When at last it does fall, it will come in savage sheets
of wetness and light from across the gorge, but in the midst
of violence, the hail will gather soft among the cottonwoods,
and the essence of sage will suffuse the smallest of souls.

The mud of the Rio Grande clings to the toes, cleaves
to the moment, won't relinquish its hold though you've flown
to the safety of cities, beheld yourself in mirrors less murky.
The absence in every storm, returns you to the source.

## Above the Gorge, Listening

Here is a silence
to humble anyone.
To confound the roar
of a restless mind.

In time, you learn
to cast that noise
into the chasm,
along with your fear.

To keep your distance
from the yearning edge.
Observe the millennia.
Let your cells respire.

Far below in the canyon,
the Rio rushes unheard
and no wind whispers
in the furnace heat.

One sound only
drags its brush across
the canvas of space:
a raven's *graw*.

## Exit, Accompanied by an Ardeid

Where else must I be
right now, really,

when a heron has landed
right here, before me,

and is content to hunt
by my side, just as long

as I can remain

blue heron still,
blue heron silent.

Nowhere, truly.

Nowhere at all.

Sun Hesper Jansen

## Full Moon and Pine

Solemn and veiled, the moon mounts the stairs
of the old white pine, as if she too is wondering:
how long?

On the ground, dead needles, red and brazen
at midday, now shine like fallen silver hair:
since when?

Haunted and cold, I list omens: brittle boughs,
and this summer, a white-spotted sawyer:
why now?

Resting, the moon tells me, enmeshed like a
tender egg in the sap-filled branches:
not yet.

## Marcescence

For seasons, we've fretted over it, this precious maple,
with its perennial mantle of perplexing desiccation,
not knowing the phenomenon has a name and perhaps
even a purpose; possibly we preferred our fancies:
you, wincing in sympathy with the naked leaves, as they
cringe and tremble and clutch each other for warmth—
me, envisioning in their moribund tenacity, a metaphor
for the American gerontocracy, fists stirred by the wind
in a mockery of vigor, denying a hold to greener shoots.
The truth is, there's no malignity in marcescence,
no omen of impending loss, no deferment of life; merely
an ecological happenstance, and a shelter for birds.

## Magnolia Knows

I've worn three coats
these past five days,

yet you, magnolia,
abide in one,

smug catkins
mocking my haste.

Very well then,
I will brew us
a pot of tea.

## March Song

The accumulation
of an age of ice
fractures,

attenuates
all patience,
stretches

to the perfect limit
of pain,

disintegrating
like sugar
on the tongue.

Shattering
in the gutter,
March rushes under

as though
she has never
truly stopped.

Sun Hesper Jansen

## Petrichor

First storm of summer
I dash from room to room
closing every window
but only just enough
to breathe at each one.

This scent had a name
before any primate spoke,
saying: here is blood
from stone, the opened
veins of the gods.

I attempt to preserve it
in apothecary bottles,
as if there were anything
more ephemeral than
the heaven of here and now.

## Fall Back

Summer jumped up
from its shallow grave
the day we gained an hour.
She was warm and spry
and only lightly
decomposed.

My mate and I
made the most of it
with a fire.
A damaged lilac
made fine kindling,
but I have a blister
to show
how unwillingly
it went.

Once again, the clocks
and calendars
cut their myths
into me, but this year
I make a wound in turn.

Listen, dead emperors:
I choose my own
day's endings.

Sun Hesper Jansen

## In the Woodpile

Searching for a ring
flung by accident
into weeds
(My hands,
my body, are
on a mission
to disappear)
I come to accept
that the earth has
swallowed it,
leaving gifts
of greater value:
a veil of diamonds,
spider-woven,
and a deadly, elegant
fungus, on which
I will feast
some other day.

*Fairy of Disenchantment*

## Lullaby for a Transplanted Herb

How fragile, your roots, dangling
between my fingers, reaching for home.
I am hardening you,
for the winter to come.

Here is a summer filament to hold
while you doze in unfamiliar soil,
in heartless light,
with the other exiles.

Strange music sends you to sleep,
but you will find your way.

Wake from slow, unbitten dreams
to find your greenness ready
for another season in the sun.

## Cold Comfort

It's a bitter night
to hunt the Huntress;
but the brittle clouds
have cleared the way
for me to glimpse her
from behind glass.

I feel as trapped
as my cat tonight,
taunted by shadows
under snow.

Last night he saw an owl
poach a fat rabbit
that should have been his.

It struck so silently.
I can still see the imprint
of its ghostly wings.

It's cold comfort,
sharing this cozy cell,
but again tonight
we dine on moonlight.

## Unseen Owls, New Year's Eve

New Year's Eve at home,
writing well past midnight,
kissing only a glass
of ice water
while snow falls.

All sound bows down
to the deadening hush
except for this:
two owls chatting
in the dark.

Reminiscing perhaps
of the year's exploits,
owlets fledged,
rodents eaten,
or simply

adoring acoustics,
astonishing writers,
magnifying silence.

# IV.
# UNDERWORLDS

sculpt  "The Sublime,"
"Who are they?"

the story   from

myths   myths and legends,

fairy tales,

long
narratives

of

shenanigans of the gods.
clouds.

## Sign at the Entrance to the Underworld

I know what you covet: deliverance
from the sun, initiation by goblin fruit.
These will be yours, thank the gods,
if you do not fear the brutal harvest.
Only travel this labyrinth, saying:
"I am home, and know my way in the dark."

Sun Hesper Jansen

## Sonata No. 6 (for Julian Scriabin)

I shiver when the work is finished,

and ask if she is pleased—knowing she
cannot answer in any human tongue.

I do not breathe until she retreats

to the silent murk, sated for now.

Such were your words, Papa—*murky,
nightmarish, and unclean*—for the
one piece that will ever appease her.

Did you know that it would fall to me,
endlessly, to feed what you released?

No longer. My music, neglected, strains
in the hollows of my skull. I wake
for days, and fear to sleep, certain now

that no choice remains but this. Today,

I will take our little skiff into the mist.

The water is black and deep here, and
there are no witnesses for what's to come.

*Fairy of Disenchantment*

Far below, the mud stirs and in that

obscure movement I hear the accursed chord.

Her gaze glitters like buried stars.

I drop to the depths, a futile bargain.
For time, for even temporary freedom,
to create what I can. There is sorrow
in her opening arms, but no mercy.
Your legacy, Papa, engulfs me.

"Sonata No. 6 (for Julian Scriabin)" was previously published in *The Chamber Magazine* (online) Jan. 22, 2021. https://thechambermagazine.com/2021/01/22/sonata-no-6-for-julian-scriabin-poem-by-sun-hesper-jansen/

## Moonchild (Mise en Abîme)

To the end I'll see you,
whirling
among the revelers,
barefoot
in a tunic of white.

In stillness, a seldom thing,
you were a slim, taut bow
in the hands of the moon.

But I saw, when you danced,
the darkness
pooling in your wake,
cast off
but forever returning.

Tragedy and death,
lithe, insatiable hounds
ran at your heels.

I made you an offer,
Lavinia,
to lift the curse,
to divert
the envy of the gods.

I offered you immortality
at the side of a prophet.
It was unwise to laugh.

Into a long scarf I wove

*Fairy of Disenchantment*

the name
of a demon reeking of
progress,
blood and gasoline.

You would not refuse
a gift from the witch
you'd made your shadow.

Only a rank acolyte
would leave
such a deed to chance.
In the mirror
I watched every moment.

How lovingly she wrapped
death around your neck.
She had no clue and no choice.

*You should wear this too,*
she said,
but you spurned her cape,
retorting:
*Je vais a l'amour!\**

As if your lust for that
Italian would warm you
all the way to hell.


He has nightmares
even now
of his responsibility, his

Sun Hesper Jansen

impotence,
witnessing your sacrifice.

The wind-borne demon reached
wildly for the axle, caught hold,
and seized me by the groin.

Hard and tight, he wrung you,
and your eyes,
wet, bulging moons, stared
right at me.
*Cyril!* you choked, three times.

Three times, like a spell,
a curse of your own, binding me
to this moment for eternity.

The demon and my ecstasy
subsided
back into the engine, back
into the mirror.
The man there was so old.

Yet I will never regret it,
deathless dancer,
corpse of moonlight,
this trap of time.
I would destroy you
again and again.

---

* 'I go to love,' said to be Isadora Duncan's last known words.

## In the Forest

Between this world and that,

a winding path lost itself
in etiolated light.

What branches remained

were unbroken. I climbed up
to a perch precarious.

There was a snap of twigs

under something fleet
but ultimately mortal.

I held my breath,

myself a tiny wildling
on four dirty paws.

It was there, as I listened

to the music of maybe,
that they appeared.

Knowing shed its pelt.

Doubt closed its eyes.
And I climbed down.

There is nothing so hungry

Sun Hesper Jansen

as possibility, nor so dire
as a strangled fantasy.

You say you can't see me

but you were whittled away,
long ago, from wondering:

What if?

## The Unseen Speaks

Never have I touched her.
I am shadow only, cold breath
for her to take into her throat.
I watch her wolf down
my feast of seeds,

paint her chin with their blood.
She has not changed.

She comes hungry, always,
to the eternal dusk.


It is tenderly revolting
the way slavering Cerberus
whines, pining for her return.
Each muzzle licks her hand.
She is gentle to them
but it takes her
a long time to lose
her estival swagger,

blend into the shades,

bear the crown's weight.

If she was gathering flowers
it was a euphemism, surely.
My Queen was a collector
of innocents, and still is.

Sun Hesper Jansen

Her torch is fueled
by supplicants like you.

To love her
is to distance yourself
from her outlandish habits.

She is my killing frost,
ever quickening winter
into fevered spring.

But the only child
she will ever carry
is our love and pity
for the living.

## The Invitation (Autumn Berries)

When did this become your calling card?
Your beacon, your in-joke, your perfume,
whose note of decay was irresistible
when we were seventeen, or younger,
willing nymphs with sugar in our hands
for the horses of the Underworld?

When did you become this other fruit?
Red and ripe amidst the leaves still falling,
against soft grass still green and fragrant,
so scandalously naked of symbolism.
What happened to that pale honeycomb
lined with crimson drops of perdition?

I know you're only waiting; soon enough
our fingers will run bloody with those seeds
and we'll gorge on preserves from hell's larder.
My hand is poised to pluck this challenge.
I try to remember that first fatal taste.
The bite of your bed of cold breezes.

I know you can wait forever; yet every year
you give me this option, open this dance
with an irresistible red invitation in your hand.
I reach toward it, like I reach for the key
you wear around your snowy neck.
A way out, whichever door I choose.

## Push it Open

Long empty, the jars, sticky with peach.
Dry, the last bottle of autumn wine,
and as we smash every glass, my tongue,
thick with congealed sweetness,
craves the astringency of spring:

bitter leaves, asparagus.
Goddess, open the door.

Long sprung, the squill and the daffodils,
and the fingers of the magnolia spread
beyond your gaunt shoulder, as you'd see
if you'd just once turn your back to me.

The sun is so strong it paints your ears
luminous rose, like a hare's.

Don't deny that you're weary of this thrall,
of feasting on dust and salted asphalt,
of your own sharp-heeled leather step,
fracturing birdsong. Admit that you hear it:

the chorus of frogs over the dirges
the dead won't let you forget.

Don't pretend that your heart didn't burst
when that hot breath from the southwest

*Fairy of Disenchantment*

kissed the back of your neck the other day.
I watched you lock away your longing

in the casket we writhe in all night.
Goddess, the key is right here.

## Danse Macabre

*N'ayons rien si souvent en la tête que la mort.* —Michel de Montaigne*

At the party, twelve lifetimes
glide past, dressed for mourning.
A dozen bright names dampened
since the crack of menarche,

not to deflect the inevitable
but to probe its secrets.

Our steps trace a map,
fictions, in place of answers.

I stand apart at the banquet,
see the bones already picked,
new courses served, new
curses as the old spells wane.

Everyone's glass rises
to honor the departing.

I will dance, but I will lead,
while my legs are limber.

Between maiden and crone
struts a hot summer stud.
The witch in the mirror laughs,
gnarled as oak, juiced to leather.

*Fairy of Disenchantment*

Bind a book with us, she says,
when our stories run out.


* 'Let us have nothing on our minds as present as death.'

Sun Hesper Jansen

## In the Second Circle, Soaring

We're supposed to burn by now
or be devoured by storms or
our own ravenous beasts.

Here is my favorite hell,
high up with Dido,
surfing the thermals

loving hard as the gale,
resting on the wing,

wondering how
we all came to be—
so blessed.

## Small Spell

I cut a leaf to carry your name.
Placed it in these waiting arms
of rosemary, so each watering
carries you on its perfume.

A small spell, for a simple gift:
a still, safe space where you
may weave your own future.

The best spells are singular: one leaf
of lemon balm, steeped with intention,
to be released from insomnia, to change
the story to one of your own telling.

May everywhere you walk, be medicine
and no meager weed without power.
A world of *pharmaka*, little and great.

Sun Hesper Jansen

## The Song of the Lindens

Lend me your voice,
god of the lindens,
for one more page.

To ride this power
to pause them in place,
to possess their senses
with memory or
sweet illusion.

Here is the first kiss
that was honest,
and here, the one
that endures.

The kiss that is refuge,
oblivion, all histories,
all selves melting
into the Beloved.

My song
is the swoon eternal,
tended with tears,
aching in dormancy.

*Fairy of Disenchantment*

In the heat of June,
let them drink in
my perfume and fall,
for anyone—
I put in their hands.

Sun Hesper Jansen

## Samhain Passage

Darkening, darkening,
the ripe land quickens.

Tiny branches, goblin fingers,
catch lovingly in my hair.

The descent is gnarled,
with alluring detours,
and the moon revealing
can easily deceive.

I follow the light in my hand,
pockets filled with seeds,
leaves, beeswax, messages
from the living world.

The blade of this time is known
to my bare feet, even in summer.

I leave crimson fox prints
all the way down.

## Trying to Work Magic at the Dawn of the Cthulhucene

I steeped the moon in a jar last night and it was good,
when I passed through the glass to a cleaner world,
to wander the silver shoreline of a lake I can still swim in,
the antipodal sister to this one.

I did not say, *What if this is a terrible idea?* Because
there was a goddess in my mind, flanked by hounds.
You have to be very careful these days, not to attract
Cyclopean horrors beyond time.

They wait so close.
Or they are already here,
driving the wrong people to suicide.

Hecate knows I am tempted. Artemis leaves arrows
lying around. The garden I cultivate could produce
one hell of a fatal brew, and speaking of that realm:
it doesn't exist, but the Darkness is real.

It is speaking to the ones who won't stop talking.
My solar-powered emergency radio is silent.
I listen to owls and katydids, and the ghosts
that walk the passages of the moon.

I hold my prism to the window,
and a breeze from another world
strokes the feathers of my face.

Sun Hesper Jansen

## Before the Wild Hunt

Rest
just a moment before we go,
you dark birds on my shoulders.
Lend me one eye each
as I contemplate the clearing
that will soon fill with howl
and rush and joyous flight.

You can lose yourself in there.
I mean to leave only the
broken bits behind.

Now
I am ready to leap headlong
into you, who fly and tumble as one,
skimming the surface of these
bodies racing through the snow,
all in pursuit of the same prey.

We have no name for it
but we all recognize
its lifeblood
on our tongues,
its purpose
in our veins.

*Fairy of Disenchantment*

## The Chord on Which the Old Year Ends

Resolution will come, I said,
when the first true snow falls.
And here it descends with
nothing settled except—
I have not yet been rejected.

The only prayers I know
are grim; may fortune
bless you with
a sustained reprieve.

I enter the blizzard searching
for a place without power lines.
The forgiving lake obliges,
but her islands of ice
are not yet for me.

I rest on the rocks,
while the swans fan
sigils into the mist
with their dingy wings.

On the way home, snow
floats into my mouth,
a surprise somehow.
It tastes like nothing.
Like stone.

Why resist unrest?
No worthy song resolves
in a major key.

Sun Hesper Jansen

Satisfaction
is ending
on a minor sixth.

*Fairy of Disenchantment*

## The Fairy Lifts Her Glass on New Year's Eve

What is left,
and what remains?

The weary glass sighs
because in its crystal
heart it knows it is
every vessel ever blown,

every one already
broken.

In this breath—
between cycles,
my glass, your glass,
overflow

with emptiness,
bubbling questions,
art and medicine,

and somewhere, always,
kindness.

# About the Author

Sun Hesper Jansen is a poet and writer of dark romantic fantasy who lives in Madison, Wisconsin.

Her work has appeared in the Indie Blu(e) anthologies *But You Don't Look Sick: The Real Life Adventures of Fibro Bitches, Lupus Warriors, and Other Superheroes Battling Invisible Illness* and *As the World Burns: Writers and Artists Reflect on a World Gone Mad*.

Her stories and poems have also appeared in *The Chamber Magazine* and *Gobblers/Masticadores*.

You can find her on Instagram @sunhesper, and on her blog, https://thefairyofdisenchantment.wordpress.com/, where she writes on/as literary therapy for Multiple Sclerosis.

# Other Indie Blu(e) Publishing Titles You Might Enjoy

# As the World Burns
## Writers and Artists Reflect on a World Gone Mad

An Indie Blu(e) Publishing Anthology

# COMPOSITION OF A WOMAN
## CHRISTINE E RAY

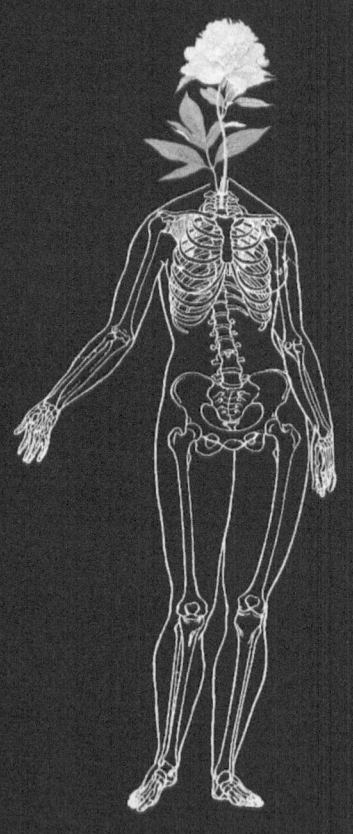

# Hospital Poems

Nancy Dunlop

Indie Blu(e) Publishing is a progressive, feminist micro-press, committed to producing honest and thought-provoking works. Our anthologies are meant to celebrate diversity and raise awareness. The editors all passionately advocate for human rights; mental health awareness; chronic illness awareness; sexual abuse survivors; and LGBTQ+ equality. It is our mission, and a great honor, to provide platforms for those voices that are stifled and stigmatized.

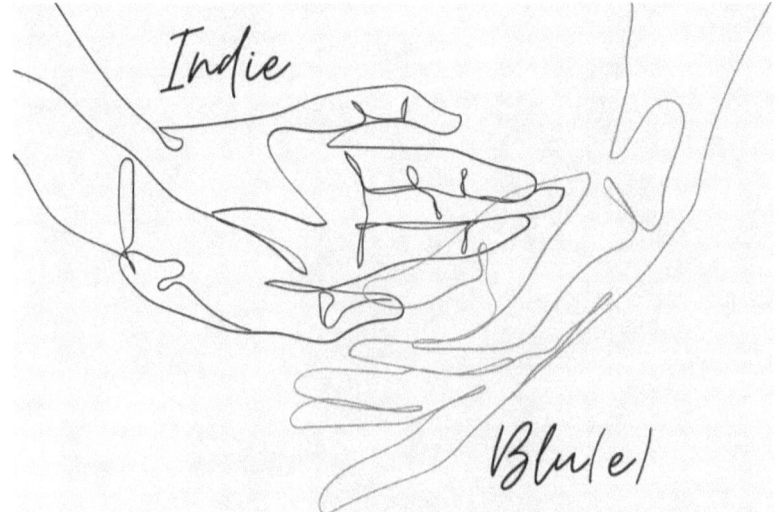

Indie Blu(e) Publishing wants your best and most incisive work. We are welcoming to all artists/writers regardless of race, orientation, gender, gender expression/identity, body type, ability, religious beliefs, income, or immigration status. We are actively seeking submissions from under-represented voices, including artists/authors who are Black, Brown, women, indigenous, gender-nonconforming, people with disabilities, lgbtqia+, and neurodivergent.

We will not accept/publish pieces that depict gratuitous violence, racism, sexism, homophobia, transphobia, xenophobia, and/or hate speech.